HEALING
RELATIONSHIPS
THROUGH FORGIVENESS

EXPERIENCING GOD'S GRACE FOR
OURSELVES

A GROUP STUDY
PART 1

DONALD E. JONES, PHD

J & A BOOK PUBLISHERS
www.jabookpublishers.com

ISBN-13: 978-0692738566
ISBN-10: 0692738568

DEDICATION

I dedicate this book to my Savior and Lord Jesus Christ. He has been with me every step of my journey upon the earth, and I so look forward to being in His presence forever and ever.

CONTENTS

ACKNOWLEDGMENTS

I want to thank my wonderful and gracious wife Carol who has supported me in this ministry with sacrifice, enthusiasm, encouragement, and accountability. Most of all, she has been a constant blessing because of her willingness to listen. I was always sharing with her the truths God had been teaching me as I studied His word and wrote this book. It consumed many hours. Thank you, Carol and I deeply love you.

I want to thank my son Gregory R. Jones for volunteering to be the primary editor of this important book. Without his time and effort in painstakingly and meticulously going over every word and every sentence checking and rechecking the sentence structure and grammar, I would not have been able to complete it. Thank you for your ministry to me. I love you my son.

I want to thank my other children, Krista, Matt, and Kara for their love for Christ and His Word and their willingness to live for Him. I love you all.

Introduction

This series of three books (Part 1,2,3) grew out of a desire to put the material in my main book on healing relationship through forgiveness into a format for small group study. As a result, the introductions are the same in all three books. This is primarily due to the essential nature of the content in our understanding of the truths found in each one. It also allows the books to be read and studied one after the other or to be studied independent of the other two. This provides more flexibility to the various individuals, groups, churches, and organizations who wish to use it.

After Moses had received the Ten Commandments, the prophet and leader requested that God show him His glory. The Almighty explained to Moses that no human could see Him and live. Nevertheless, God would grant his request by allowing His servant Moses to experience the passing of His "goodness" by him and the actual viewing of the "backside of His glory." On the next morning, he stood upon a rock and called upon the name of the Lord. The Lord God descended in the form of a cloud, shielded Moses in the cleft of the rock, and covered him with His divine hand. As God displayed His divine glory visibly, He declared the many attributes of His supernatural, divine character.

In Exodus 34:6-7, Moses described this amazing moment and the words that he heard the Lord declare about Himself. The prophet recorded, "Yahweh [I AM THAT I AM] passed by before him...he proclaimed, 'Yahweh! Yahweh, a merciful and gracious God, slow to anger...abundant in His loving kindness and truth, keeping loving kindness for thousands, forgiving iniquity and disobedience and sin.'" A book that is written on healing relationships through forgiveness by its nature must begin with the proclamation that the God of the universe is not only the merciful, gracious, patient, loving, kind, truth-filled, just, and righteous Lord but an Almighty deity who "forgives iniquity, transgressions, and sin." This Lord God announced that He is a "forgiving" God.

This by no means negates the fact that He is also a just and righteous one; therefore, this forgiveness comes with a price that had to be paid. So, He sent His Son to die to pay the penalty for our sins in order to pour out His forgiveness upon all mankind. Through faith in Jesus Christ, men and women experience the full extent of His forgiveness that was proclaimed to Moses many years ago on that mountain top. Once this has occurred in our lives, we are to live for Him. We are to act like Him, and we are to obey Him. One of the critical ways in which God desires His forgiven people to live for, act like, and obey Him is *to forgive others as we are forgiven*. This is the key point of these books. As the Lord God has forgiven us and healed our relationship with Him, He requires us to forgive and heal our relationships with others. This is found in several passages in the Scriptures. Two of them are mentioned by our Lord and one from the apostle Paul. All three clearly explain the important truth that relationships are to be "reconciled" and "restored" to "gain back" one's brother, sister, or neighbor. This is done primarily through forgiveness.

In Matthew 5, the Lord Jesus discusses the heart attitudes people in His kingdom should possess. After speaking of anger, the Lord presents a general principle of living in His kingdom on earth. In verses 23-24, He explains, "If therefore you are offering your gift at the altar, and there remember that your brother has anything against you, leave your gift there before the altar, and go your way. First be reconciled to your brother, and then come and offer your gift." The Greek word translated "reconciled" means "to make changes." It originates from a Greek root word that was a banking term meaning "to render accounts the same." There would be a discrepancy between two bank ledgers, and all the mistakes would have to be found and corrected in order for them to agree. We express this between people as "being on the same page." The Lord Jesus indicates that the Father desires His people to come to Him fully reconciled with each other. If we, as Christians, know that someone harbors something against us, we are to take the initiative and go to them and reconcile with them. We should not wait for them to come to us. We take our responsibility and go to them. We must once again "settle accounts." They have the same responsibility.

In Matthew 18, Jesus discusses those who are sinning in the church and what all believers should do. In verse 15, the Lord commands, "If your brother sins against you, go, show him his fault between you and him alone. If he listens to you, you have gained back your brother." The Greek word translated "gain" refers "to obtaining or securing something." When a relationship is restored, we gain back everything that the other parties contributed. In this particular case, we have something against our brother, rather than the reverse. If this does happen, we are to take the initiative and confront our brother or sister to gain him or her back and restore the relationship. So whether someone has something against us or we have something against someone else, the procedure is essentially the same. Christians must take the initiative and reconcile with them.

The third passage involves the restoration of a sinning brother in the church. In Galatians 6, Paul opens the chapter with an explanation of how to help a sinning saint. In verse one, Paul asserts, "Brothers, even if a man is caught in some fault, you who are spiritual must restore such a one." The Greek word translated "restore" means "to render fit, sound, or complete; to mend or repair what has been broken." The word is used of a physically broken fishing net. In Mark 1:19

and Matthew 4:21, when Jesus called James and John into ministry with Him, they were in the process of "mending" their fishing nets. They were mending the holes in their net so the fish would not fall through. This restoration could easily involve a conflict between two people. The holes in their relationship need to be mended. This process involves healing relationships through forgiveness. These passages will be referred to as you read.

These books are my original works on reconciliation and forgiveness. It is not based on other books that I have read and simply collated. To produce this work, I carefully read through the entire New Testament verse by verse. Then, I meticulously perused the Old Testament paying particular attention to the Psalms and Proverbs. As I read, categories were built from the individual passages, rather than a set of preconceived notions. These numerous categories became the individual biblical principles found in every chapter. Each passage was studied in its historical, grammatical, and scriptural contexts. After this, I compared my interpretations with those of past and present scholars. After this study, I have attempted to follow these biblical principles in my own personal life and also utilize them in my pastoral counseling practice. I have seen the Holy Spirit use them to transform relationships of all kinds.

One last thought. At the end of each chapter, I discuss a counseling experience. Due to confidentiality, none of these are based on one particular counseling situation. Instead, I have mixed together common elements I have seen, details from books and films, bits from my own life and the lives of people I have known, and thoughts from my imagination to create a situation where the biblical principles discussed in the chapters can fully be applied. These are composites of real life situations. Read, learn, and apply. I commend you to the Lord and His Word (Acts 20:32).

Chapter 1

Involve God First

The first important step in the reconciliation process is the recognition that no matter who else we have sinned against, we have sinned against our God first. Therefore, when we have transgressed someone, we must initially ask God for forgiveness and reconcile with Him before we reconcile with others (see Introduction). It is His law that was broken.

A Typical Scenario

Have you ever had or heard a conversation with a spouse, parent, child, or friend that went something like this? You say or hear, "Oh, I will also tell you something else! (Person responds.) No, that is not the way it was! (Person responds again.) No, that is what you think it was, but it is not at all the way we had decided! (Person responds again.) No, I'm not going to do it that way! (Person responds again.) No, at the very beginning we did not decide to do it that way!"

Even as we are arguing, we know thirty minutes later the conviction of the Holy Spirit in us will come upon us. As we expected, the argument is over, and no one has won. We are sitting alone reviewing the conversation in our minds in a self-righteous state blaming the other person. Then the Holy Spirit begins His convicting work in our hearts. We think, "Okay, maybe we contributed to the argument." Then we stop ourselves and realize that we actually started the whole argument in the first place. Either way, we must return to the person we transgressed and work things out with them. This is God's will; yet, this is not the first step.

5

A Scriptural Principle

Before we take the important step of reconciling with the person, we must first ask our God for forgiveness. The first principle in the forgiveness and reconciliation process is "we must recognize that our sin is first against God." Yes, we are arguing with our spouse, parent, friend, or neighbor, and we have violated that relationship but that's not the first issue. Our relationship with Almighty God, our relationship with our Master and Lord comes first, and we have transgressed Him as we transgressed the other person.

A Biblical Explanation

As we are arguing with our spouse, parent, or friend, we are actually disrupting our relationship with God first. Why? It is His standards and laws that we are violating. Therefore, before we can go to our spouses we must deal with Him. This is found in Psalm 51. David has just committed the sins of adultery and murder which have been exposed. David opens the psalm crying out for God's mercy. He begs God for the forgiveness of these horrible transgressions and asks Him to wash him thoroughly from these sins and make him clean again. Then in Psalm 51:4, David utters, "Against you, and you only, have I sinned, and done that which is evil in your sight; that you may be proved right when you speak, and justified when you judge."

The word translated "only" in the English does not refer to God as the only one transgressed. Instead, it has the idea of "separate from." David is stating that His transgression against God is completely separate, wholly different, and stands alone when compared to anyone else that has been transgressed. He had sinned against Bathsheba, Uriah, their families, and even the nation of Israel as their leader, but this cannot be compared to the gravity and the seriousness of his sin against God. Why? God is above all else in the universe (Psalm 115:3). He is the ruler of all nations (Psalm 22:28) and the sovereign God (Ephesians 1:11). God is the law giver, and His law has been transgressed (James 2:10; 4:12). Most of all, His Son is our Lord (Romans 10:12-13). He was present listening to the conversation as we argued. He stands before us in every transgression. He must be asked for forgiveness.

The others transgressed do not set standards of behavior. God alone does. The Lord must be dealt with on a separate and utterly divine level before all others in the transgression. In Psalm 41:4, David again takes up the lament of his sins which brought reprisal from his enemies. The king cries, "I said, 'Yahweh, have mercy on me! Heal me, for I have sinned against you.'" Then this great king paints a beautiful picture of the relief he experiences in forgiveness. In Psalm 41:11-13, he shouts, "By this I know that you delight in me, because my enemy doesn't triumph over me. As for me, you uphold me in my integrity, and set me in your presence forever. Blessed be Yahweh, the God of Israel, from everlasting and to everlasting! Amen and amen."

As Solomon is dedicating the temple he had just built for God, He brings the sins of his people before the Holy One. The king begs God for their forgiveness as he anticipates the many prayers that will proceed from this new structure. In 2 Chronicles 6:21, he asserts, "Listen to the petitions of your servant, and of your people Israel, when they shall pray toward this place: yes, hear from your dwelling place, even from heaven; and when you hear, forgive." Then in verse 25, he adds, "Forgive the sin of your people Israel." In verse 27, he continues, "Then hear in heaven, and forgive the sin of your servants." In the same prayer in verse 39, he repeats, "Then hear from heaven, even from your dwelling place, their prayer and their petitions, and maintain their cause, and forgive your people who have sinned against you." Here in the great temple dedication, Solomon recognizing the constant and continual sin of his people. When they come before God in prayer, they must recognize their sin and repent before God. When transgressions occur, they are first against God, and this must be acknowledged.

In Psalm 79:9, the psalmist cries, "Help us, God of our salvation, for the glory of your name. Deliver us, and forgive our sins, for your name's sake." Here again is this requesting of forgiveness by God's children as expressed by the writer. This is critical in understanding the reconciliation process with others. We must reconcile with God first because He is the Supreme Being and His Son is Lord and Master of our lives. In Matthew 6, the disciples asked Jesus to frame a prayer for them to follow. In verse 12, Jesus uttered, "Forgive us our debts, as we also forgive our debtors." An essential part of our prayers is asking God the Father for forgiveness. What an amazing thing it is to be able to come before our loving God and ask for forgiveness! When we arrive at His throne in prayer as His children, we will find a God who is ready, willing, and able to forgive any transgression! No one understood this better than King David.

In Acts 7, Stephen, one of the mighty witnesses of Christ, stood before the Jewish governing body, the Sanhedrin, and preached a powerful message of salvation. In Acts 7:54, Luke described their reaction in these words, "Now when they heard these things, they were cut to the heart, and they gnashed at him with their teeth." Then in verses 57-58, Luke added, "But they cried out with a loud voice, and stopped their ears, and rushed at him with one accord. They threw him out of the city, and stoned him. The witnesses placed their garments at the feet of a young man named Saul." This Saul, who would become Paul, watched Stephen's life pass out of him with great anticipation and full agreement. From that day forward, Saul set out to destroy the church of Jesus Christ which had just been established.

Luke describes Saul as "ravaging" the church. He went from house to house dragging off Christian men and women and had them thrown in prison. As the saints were scattered because of the persecution, Saul followed them breathing threats and murder against them. Finally, he obtained letters from the Sanhedrin to travel some 135 miles to Damascus to find more Christians, have them bound with the help of the local synagogue, and drag them back to Damascus to have them tried and killed. Most Christians know the story. On that road to Damascus, Saul was confronted by Jesus Christ, saved, and commissioned to be a servant of God. Sometime after Saul, the persecutor, became Paul, the apostle, he was reflecting back on his early days of terror. As the apostle wrote to young Timothy, a trusted companion and fellow pastor, he remembered the horrific affliction he had brought upon those innocent Christians and the mercy he received in God's forgiveness.

In 1 Timothy 1:12-15, the apostle characterizes himself as a blasphemer, persecutor, aggressor, and the foremost of all sinners. Then in verses 14-15, the apostle describes the open arms of God in forgiveness as he came in repentance. Paul writes, "The grace of our Lord abounded exceedingly with faith and love which is in Christ Jesus. The saying is faithful and worthy of all acceptance, that Christ Jesus came into the world to save sinners; of whom I am chief." The Lord came into the world to die so He could open His arms to us in abundant grace! In verse 16, Paul adds, "However, for this cause I obtained mercy, that in me first, Jesus Christ might display all his patience, for an example of those who were going to believe in him for eternal life." The apostle became a powerful and shining example of God's patience as He calls people to Himself through His grace and mercy. Once saved, we still find Him gracious and merciful as we confess our sins to Him.

Paul continues to marvel at the grace, love, and mercy he experienced as he came before the Lord in repentance. No matter how heinous is the transgression, how disgusting is the sin, or even how atrocious is the iniquity, when we come before almighty God, His arms are outstretched, his hands are open, and His heart is ready to forgive. His grace, mercy, and love will outpour into forgiveness when we come to confess our sins. Our God is a Father who is always ready to forgive.

After the people of Israel had been disciplined for seventy years in captivity, God released them from the Persians, and they once again entered the land. Once the wall was rebuilt and they were safe, they reinstated the celebration of the Feast of Booths. All the people gathered together and read from the Scriptures for a full quarter of the day and then confessed their sins and worshipped the Lord for another quarter. Then in Nehemiah 9:17, a group of priests stood up and reviewed the evil of their fathers in this way, "And [the fathers] refused to obey, neither were they mindful of your wonders that you did among them, but hardened their neck, and in their rebellion appointed a captain to return to their bondage." Then they add God's forgiveness, "But you are a God ready to pardon, gracious and merciful, slow to anger, and abundant in loving kindness, and didn't forsake them."

When we sin against God, He never forsakes us. Instead, God waits in readiness for our return to Him in repentance and confession. David acknowledges this in his Psalm 86:5, when the king wrote, "For you, Lord, are good, and ready to forgive; abundant in loving kindness to all those who call on you." This God of ours is ready to forgive when we sin. He is full of love and kindness to all who call upon Him. Then in verse 8, he shouts, "There is no one like you among the gods, Lord, nor any deeds like your deeds." In the midst of God's willingness to forgive, He only demands that we come to Him first to reconcile our relationships. He is our Lord; we must humble ourselves before Him in repentance, before we humble ourselves before others.

An Ancient Portrait

David was a mighty man of God, but he struggled with his passions. This led sometimes to terrible wickedness. His most infamous sin against God occurred in 2 Samuel 11-12. King David was the second ruler of Israel and a great King. In the days of good weather, Israel would go out to battle. In one such battle, David remained in Jerusalem. One evening the king was up on the roof of his palace relaxing (the roof was used in that part of the world much like a backyard patio is used in the western world). He noticed a beautiful woman bathing in the privacy of her home and wanted her.

David was king and could have any woman he wanted whenever he wanted her. So, he commanded his servants to bring her to him. He was the king, and she could not refuse. After he had his way with Bathsheba, David sent her home expecting absolutely no consequences. Sometime later, one of her messengers arrived and she told the foolish king that Bathsheba was pregnant. Now, what would David be able to do? Of course, he would try the first thing many people do when they are caught which is to cover it up. So, a clever idea came to him. He would call Uriah, her husband and a soldier, back from the battlefield. When he returned, Uriah would sleep with Bathsheba and think her child was his; the king directed his commander Joab to return Uriah to him. After greeting David, Uriah was sent home. The king fully expected Uriah to enjoy the fruits of his marriage.

This loyal and faithful soldier refused to enter his home while his fellow warriors were in battle. Instead, he slept at the door of the king's house with the king's servants. When his majesty was informed that Uriah did not return home, he summoned the man and questioned him. Uriah responded by indicating that he could not take any pleasures while the Ark of Israel's God was under siege. It was inconceivable to him that he should rest while his fellow soldiers fought for their lives. It was simply not be respectable.

Now what was the king going to do? David conjured up another plan; he would invite Uriah to stay in his palace for the night and enjoy a magnificent meal with much drinking. Once her husband was fully intoxicated, the man would lose this silly notion and sleep with his wife as David had. The Scriptures indicate that King David made him drunk. This monarch probably insisted that Uriah continue to drink, even over the husband's protests. When Uriah finally left, David felt assured that his plan would work. Once again, the king underestimated this soldier of his. Even in his drunken state, Uriah refused to return to his home. He was not going to enjoy his wife and home when his fellow soldiers were in battle. Instead, he stayed with David's servants.

At this point, David was done with his attempts to coerce this man to sleep with his own wife. The king commanded Uriah to resume his duties on the battlefield. The soldier was given a letter to personally hand to Joab, the commander of David's troops. In that letter was the King's final scheme and Uriah's death knell. Joab was to assign this obstinate soldier to the front lines of battle. At an opportune time, the troops around him would withdraw, and Uriah would be killed in battle. This will make it look like Uriah was a war hero, leave Bathsheba a widow, and allow David to take her as his wife. He would be able to raise this child without disgrace. This would be the perfect solution to his dilemma.

When the news came that Uriah had been killed, it was finally over. The problem had been solved. King David must have sighed in relief. After the time of Bathsheba's mourning was over, she became David's wife. All of this was done as if the Lord had not been around. All along the way, God must have been too busy with other things to even notice what he had done. Big problem! God Almighty had viewed the entire mess, and it was evil in His sight. When no one was looking, God was still there. When secret plans were being made and executed, God was present, and His laws were being broken.

Sometime later, Nathan, God's prophet, entered David's palace with a story to tell the great king. It was time to indict David for his foul play before the Lord. Nathan stood before David to seek his advice concerning a situation that he had encountered between two different men. Nathan described a city where two men lived, a rich man and a poor man. This rich man had much wealth, but the poor man had only one little ewe lamb. The poor man loved this lamb and treated it like his own child. When a traveler arrived and resided at the house of the rich man, a lavish meal had to be prepared and served. Rather than taking his own lamb, the rich man took the poor man's lamb, cooked it up, and served it.

King David did not even wait for the prophet to finish his story. He immediately declared that the rich man should be killed. Before he was to die, the man should make restitution fourfold for what he had done. Nathan stared directly at the king and declared that David was the rich man in his story. With this recognition of David's heinous sin came a series of judgments pronounced upon David from God Himself. How could David have done such a thing before God? It is easy he just pretended God was not there. Yet, He was. After this incident, King David repented of these sins and asked God for forgiveness. This is when he penned the inspired words of Psalm 51. This is a powerful prayer of repentance.

He did not initially rush off to reconcile with Bathsheba, her family or Uriah's, or anyone else involved. First, he had to face His Lord God. When we sin against someone, we must recognize we have sinned against God and reconcile with Him. Once this occurs, we can concern ourselves with others. In fact, we will have the right heart and mind to be truly humble enough to reconcile with them.

A Modern Anecdote

Sometime ago, a married couple came into my counseling office to discuss a drinking problem his wife had. It came to a boiling point when the husband found his wife lying on the front lawn of his house in the morning. She was wearing her pajamas, and the lawn sprinklers were running. She was almost completely unconscious and not aware she was even getting wet. He helped her get up, and she stumbled into the house. Eventually, they got into a huge argument accusing one another of instigating the drunken behavior in the first place. As with many issues in relationships each contributed to the wife's constant drinking in different ways.

It turns out that the husband was always annoyed at her for a variety of habits she had constantly displayed during their marriage. As a result, he would pick at her and criticize her for many of the things she did. He did not like the way she left the dishes on the sink to dry or how she folded the towels. The house was not clean enough for his tastes. The list just went on and on. Rather than discussing the situation with him, the wife drank and drank. The more he picked on her, the more she drank. The more she drank, the more he criticized and picked on her. Until finally all of it had gotten so out of control, their marriage was on the line. Now, their divorce was eminent. As they faced each other in my office, they felt justified in their behavior.

After several intense sessions, I discovered the underlying drama that had motivated these actions. I stood them face to face before the Lord. He was their Savior and Master. What did Jesus think about their behavior (according to the Bible)? Once in front of the Lord, their inappropriate actions came to light. Both partners had brought into their marriage different approaches to washing dishes, the laundry, their cars, and cleaning the house among other issues.

The Scriptures do not speak to many of the issues directly but do indicate that both partners must love, respect, and understand each other (Ephesians 5:33; 1 Peter 3:7). Neither partner was taking the necessary time to listen to the other one. Instead, the husband continually argued and the wife constantly drank. Differences between people can never be resolved through yelling and drinking. The Scriptures are clear that believers are not to argue or quarrel (2 Timothy 2:24; Proverbs 18:19; 20:3; 22:10) and Christians are never to be drunk (Ephesians 5:18; Romans 13:13; Psalm 69:12). This approach dishonored the Lord. This is not how Jesus Christ desires couples, who are fellow heirs of the grace of life, to behave toward each other (1 Peter 3:7). Instead, the Lord expects them to treat each other as He treats His own church (Ephesians 5:23,25,31).

After several sessions, each one could now see what their responsibility was in the relationship and how they had to behave. This required apologizing, accepting the repentance, and beginning again. Yet, the Lord could not be left out. He comes first. I sent them to the Father to reconcile with Him. Though they had hurt each other, they were hurting Him first. His laws had been broken, and they were not following His Word. Today, they are living with each other in a more mutually loving, understanding, and respectful way before the Lord. The husband has stopped his yelling, and the wife has stopped her responding with alcohol.

They have found real harmony and unity as they work out their differences together. The key to the resolution to this entire problem was to stand before our God and answer to Him first. When we think we are only accountable to our spouses or others, then it is easy to continue the sinful and inappropriate behaviors and not reconcile. When the Lord God, master of our lives, enters the conflict, then our minds become clear and the right response will come through the Holy Spirit. So often, Christians in their many relationships fail to consider Christ as the Lord of their relationship. When they focus on each other alone, anything can happen.

A Personal Response

Dear Heavenly Father,

When I was sinning against (add name), I did not realize that I was first and foremost sinning against You. I did not recognize that You were right there with me, and Your laws were being transgressed. I am deeply sorry for all the sinful thoughts, words, and actions I have committed toward (add name) which were against You too. I have transgressed Your righteous law. Help me to reconcile with (add name) so we may honor and glorify You. I pray this in the name of Jesus. Amen.

Chapter 2

Leave Nothing Out

In the first chapter, we learned we must recognize that we are sinning against God first. Therefore, we should reconcile with Him before attempting to reconcile with the person we may have wronged in a relationship. As we walk into God's presence to ask for forgiveness, we must realize God knows the entire story and every detail of what we have done. As we confess our transgressions, we must admit to all of them holding nothing back.

A Typical Scenario

Have you ever had or heard a phone conversation with a customer representative that went something like this? You say or hear, "No! The item that you gave me is not working. First, I talked to you, and then you put me on hold, and sent me to somebody else. She also put me on hold and sent me to another person, and he placed me on hold while I was talking. Then, I was disconnected. I had to call back! This is the third time I have called about this same exact problem. Obviously, none of you know what you are doing! (Person responds.) Okay! Fine! Goodbye!"

We all have had this kind of interaction with a customer service representative of a company. Then sometime later, we suddenly start feeling guilty for how poorly we treated the representative. Then we think, "Well, nobody saw it. Nobody is here. Nobody is around! So what is the harm?" This couldn't be further from the truth. There is one person who sees everything that we do. He is the invisible observer of all our good and evil behavior, and nothing escapes His gaze. This person is God. We may attempt to conceal a small or minute detail of what we did to others we have hurt in a relationship, but we cannot hide it from our Father. We may think unkind thoughts about people, even say something evil to someone about them, or do something in secret that is against them, but God sees it all. When we ask Him for forgiveness, these should not be left out. Everything should be confessed as the Holy Spirit brings them to mind.

A Scriptural Principle

The second principle is "we must know that God knows all our sins, so we must own up to all of them." Sometimes, when we go to ask for forgiveness from someone, we do not want to accept all of the responsibility we had in the sin. We want to leave out some of the words or actions which may embarrass us the most or lessen our responsibility. At other times, we like to alter the story slightly to make us look a little better; this is not the way God deals with things. God desires us to confess to Him everything we said or did, not just what we might feel is expedient, convenient, or even less embarrassing to us.

A Biblical Explanation

There might be times, where it would be too hurtful and not edifying to disclose everything we thought or may have said in private to someone we have wronged, but we should confess these to God. As a result, when we confess our sins and ask for forgiveness from the ones we wronged, none of the important details will be left out. We should take the true responsibility for what happened as we go before the throne of our God in prayer.

Confession before God involves the acknowledgement of all our sin. In Psalm 32:3-4, David describes the torment he felt when he refused to confess all his sins and kept them bottled up inside. He sobs, "When I kept silence, my bones wasted away through my groaning all day long. For day and night your hand was heavy on me. My strength was sapped in the heat of summer. Selah." Then in the next verse, he finally acknowledges all his sin. In Psalm 32:5, he continues, "I acknowledged my sin to you. I didn't hide my iniquity. I said, I will confess my transgressions to Yahweh, and you forgave the iniquity of my sin. Selah." Then the king paints a beautiful picture of the relief that he experiences. In Psalm 32:11, David adds this, "Be glad in Yahweh, and rejoice, you righteous! Shout for joy, all you who are upright in heart!"

When Solomon cried out to God for the forgiveness of his people, it was for all their transgressions. In 1 Kings 8:50, he proclaimed these powerful words, "And forgive your people who have sinned against you, and all their transgressions in which they have transgressed against you; and give them compassion before those who carried them captive, that they may have compassion on them." We must admit every detail of what happened between us and the person or persons we have transgressed. God wants all confessed before Him.

In Psalm 90:8, Moses acknowledges this when he asserts, "You have set our iniquities before you, our secret sins in the light of your presence." Both Moses and the nation of Israel had a problem with sin, and he states that their iniquities and sin were before the Lord, even the hidden ones. These secret transgressions that no one knows are exposed in the light of God's presence. The light of God's holiness brings to light all our sins, even the ones hidden from all. Moses is explaining that the Lord sees all our sins. No iniquity can be hidden from Him. Once we are cognizant of His continual presence, His light exposes our sin.

God even knows the transgressions we do not realize we have committed. In Psalm 19:12, David declares, "Who can discern his errors?" Then the king cries, "Forgive me from hidden errors." When no one knows, even ourselves, a sin that we have committed, still our God knows! Then in Psalm 69:5, David cries out, "God, you know my foolishness. My sins aren't hidden from you." In Psalm 44, the sons of Korah describe how God's people had fallen into idolatry. In verses 20-21, they exclaimed, "If we have forgotten the name of our God, or spread out our hands to a strange god; won't God search this out? For he knows the secrets of the heart." God knows all that happened, and it cannot be hidden from him.

In Proverbs 15:3, King Solomon characterizes God in this way, "Yahweh's eyes are everywhere, keeping watch on the evil and the good." While God is keeping watch, our Father is pleased or displeased with what He sees. In verse 26, the king writes, "Yahweh detests the thoughts of the wicked, but the thoughts of the pure are pleasing." So not only is God viewing all our behavior but actually judging it according to His standards. He is watching how we treat the people we interact with in our lives.

Since God can look deeply into the recesses of our hearts and minds, He can also clearly see our motives and reasons for our behavior toward others. In Proverbs 17:3, Solomon adds, "The refining pot is for silver, and the furnace for gold, but Yahweh tests the hearts." In Proverbs 16:2, the wise king declared, "All the ways of a man are clean in his own eyes; but Yahweh weighs the motives." As God is weighing our hearts, we may see some thought, word, or action as of no account or even righteous, but God may judge it differently. He may see it as evil.

Why do we often attempt to cover up the evil we do from God? He knows us completely. In Psalm 139:4, David cries aloud, "For there is not a word on my tongue, but, behold, Yahweh, you know it altogether." Even before any word is spoken by us, it is already before His eyes. Nothing can be hidden, everything must be confessed (if we know about it). When we start the process of reconciliation, we all must first recognize that we have transgressed God's law and should confess everything to Him.

So we must go before God with every thought, word, and action and lay them bare before Him. How do we do this? Through prayer, we ask the Holy Spirit to convict us of any transgression in the breakup of the relationship that we have committed. One of the responsibilities of the Holy Spirit in our lives is to convict us of sin (John 16:8). How does He do this? In Psalm 139:23-24, David beseeches, "Search me, God, and know my heart. Try me, and know my thoughts." Then he adds, "See if there is any wicked way in me, and lead me in the everlasting way." He entreats the Lord to show Him where he has failed.

Can we imagine the power of asking the Lord to convict us of our responsibility in an incident in our relationship with a spouse, parent, friend, fellow student, teacher, or co-worker? Are we not always reviewing in our minds what they did, when we should really be reviewing what we did! As we are engaging in this prayer, we should be searching the Scripture. Conviction will come from the Holy Spirit through the truth of the Word of God.

In Hebrews 4:12, the author of Hebrews explains, "For the word of God is living and active, and sharper than any two-edged sword, piercing even to the dividing of soul and spirit, of both joints and marrow, and is able to discern the thoughts and intentions of the heart." The Scriptures can dig deep into our very hearts and discern thoughts, motives, and intentions. Then God will convict us of them.

In 2 Timothy 2:7, Paul exhorted Timothy, his son in the faith, to be a gentle, yet strong shepherd of God; then, Paul adds this request, "Consider what I say, and may the Lord give you understanding in all things." Paul was confident that the Lord would help him understand everything he had told him, including where he had gone wrong and how he could correct the situation. In Psalm 119:169, thousands of years ago, the psalmist proclaimed, "Let my cry come before you, Yahweh. Give me understanding according to your word." He knew that God's Word would convict him as he cried out to the Lord God. In Psalm 119:175-176, this psalm ends with these beautiful words, "Let my soul live, that I may praise you. Let your ordinances help me. I have gone astray like a lost sheep. Seek your servant, for I don't forget your commandments." When we go astray, these commands in His Word guide us back.

The best way to do this is to go step by step through every thought, word, and action in the transgression. We should judge each one according to the Word and depend on the Holy Spirit to guide us. Notice, we go through our actions, not the other person's. Often, when we recount a falling out between us and others, we carefully judge their thoughts (inferred by us), words, and actions; then, we get angrier and angrier, sometimes even letting ourselves off the hook in the light of their transgression. This is not God's way. We are responsible for our actions before God, not theirs.

An Ancient Portrait

In Genesis 1-3, we are given the story of Adam and Eve as they walked with the Lord God in the Garden of Eden and their subsequent fall from His grace. God created man and placed him in a garden. Adam was given the responsibility to name the animals and subdue the earth. God told Adam that He could eat of all trees of the garden, except for the Tree of the Knowledge of Good and Evil. As Adam named the animals, it became evident there was not a companion suitable for him as there was in the animal kingdom. The Lord God saw that it was not good for Adam to be alone and proceeded to create a woman for him. God put Adam into a deep sleep and then took from his body one of his ribs, and formed that into a companion for him.

When Adam awoke he declared that the woman was now bone of his bones and flesh of his flesh. As a result, a man is to leave his father and mother and cleave to his wife. They will join together and become one flesh. This is when God created marriage. While Adam and Eve were in the garden and enjoying its many fruits and God's presence, suddenly a serpent appeared. We know that this was the Devil, but Eve did not know. The Serpent asked Eve about the Tree of the Knowledge of Good and Evil. When she said that it would essentially kill them if they ate of it, he disagreed. Instead, he told Eve that if she ate of it, her eyes would be opened, and she would be like God. Nice thought! Be Divine! Big Lie!

So Eve looked at the tree. She saw that it was good for food; it delighted her eyes and would make her wise like God. She grabbed its fruit and ate. Then she handed it over to Adam and he ate it also. Suddenly, they realized that they were naked. Why? For the first time, they understood lust and evil desire, so they sought to cover themselves with leaves. They wanted to remove the shame they felt at being naked. Then they heard God coming. Now what were they going to do? Of course, they decided to hide from God.

They wanted to conceal their sin from God. So off to the bushes they went. Did they really think they could get away with this? Yes. Do we really think we can hide our sin from an all-knowing God? Yes, we really do. We fool ourselves by simply committing the sin without any thoughts of God. Put Him out of our mind while we fight, argue, yell, scream at someone and pick Him up later on. Perhaps, this is exactly what Adam and Eve also did. Where were their thoughts of God while they were being tempted?

Of course, God knows exactly where they are. God knows everything. He began making sounds as He approached, so the couple would know He was on His way. This was their first chance to admit to everything they had done. Instead, they hid themselves because the two were naked. They were more concerned about the situation of their nakedness, then the fact that they had just transgressed the Lord God. Are we not like that? We can get so wrapped up in the situation; we forget He is right there being transgressed.

Then the Lord God called to Adam and asked him where he was. Here God provided another opportunity for them to spring forth from their hiding place and admit all they had done. Instead, Adam explains that they had hid themselves because they were naked. God then inquired as to how they knew they were naked and whether they had eaten from the tree. Adam responded with man's first real excuse for his sin which will lead to a long history of excuses. Adam blamed the Lord and His wife. His wife blamed the Serpent who had tricked her.

There is a whole lot of finger-pointing at each other not at themselves. Adam blames the Lord God for giving him the woman in the first place. This action created the whole mess. The woman, Eve, blames the Serpent for his trickery. It was entirely someone else's fault; of course they would think that as we do. Though not really mentioned directly, we know they admitted all of their sins, but the damage had already been done. The human race had fallen into sin which would lead to both physical and eternal death.

Believe me, we all have our excuses why the relationship was fouled up, and it is never our fault! We are the victims! Had our wives, husbands, sons, daughters, fathers, mothers, friends, acquaintances, co-workers, fellow students, or even customer service representatives acted any differently, we would not have reacted the way we did! Does this not sound familiar? We want to always be the victim! If we can blame someone else, we do not have to carry the full guilt for the destruction of the relationship. Unfortunately, that doesn't work for God, and it did not work for Adam and Eve. God desires people to take responsibility for their sins. He will not take any excuses.

A Modern Anecdote

Many of my male clients have struggled with the evil of pornography. One such husband came to my office with his wife livid over his many mental affairs. While weeping, she recounted the evening she had found him in a compromised position lounging at his computer. As her emotions flooded out of her, he sat slumped over with his head down quietly muttering how difficult this all was and how embarrassed he felt. It was an utterly sad day for their relationship, but they desired to overcome this predicament with God's help. They both wanted a strong marriage once again. They had entered into a lifetime covenant and were determined to remain in it.

Unfortunately, this problem can have multiple reasons for the issue to begin and multiple different reasons for the issue to have continued. It took some time to fully discover all of the factors involved and the extent to which the husband had actually sinned. Needless to say, pornography is a sin of the heart. It is sexual immorality of the heart (Matthew 5:28; 1 Corinthians 6:18; Galatians 5:19). There were many nights and more websites than he could even recall.

As I met with him individually, he was even too ashamed to disclose the full extent of what he had seen, nor could he admit everything he had done to his dear wife. Neither was actually necessary. This believer was accountable to His God first, and He would confess all of it to Him and Him alone. I did not need to know every detail to help him and his dear wife did not need to be traumatized by all that he had done, since it was confined to his computer and the images alone.

Yet, to begin their healing process, this husband had to acknowledge that God had been there all along and he had done such evil in His presence. I will always remember that day he cried to the Lord in my office mumbling silently his sorrow while confessing the minute details of His sin to His Savior and Lord as I sat next to him praying. The man knew that Jesus Christ was forgiving him even as he was uttering quietly his many transgressions.

Then the healing process was initiated with his wife as he confessed to her his sins, and she forgave him. Over a course of time, these unrighteous practices were put away and fully replaced with holy ones that honored the Lord (Galatians 5:19-25; Ephesians 4:25-32). He battled with his flesh to keep from stumbling, and she battled with hers to fully forgive him.

Eventually, victory came on both their parts, and the issue was finally settled in their relationship. I must mention one last thing. During the process, the man's wife realized that some things she did and did not do concerning their sexual interactions contributed to his problem. She realized that she perhaps had not fulfilled all of her responsibilities sexually to her husband (1 Corinthians 7:1-5). This contributed to his sexually charged state when the woman's advances began. Though this was difficult to bear and not an excuse for his sin, she asked the Lord and her husband for forgiveness.

A Personal Response

Dear Heavenly Father,

I recognize you are present everywhere I go and view everything I do. While I was reading this chapter, I realized that I have kept back from confessing all of the sins that I committed against (add name). I now confess them to You (list them). I am so sorry. I have transgressed your holy and righteous law. Please give me the courage to admit all my wrongs to (add name). Help me to honor and glorify You in my relationship with (add name) and follow your Word. I pray this in the name of Jesus. Amen.

Chapter 3

Admit Your Sin

When we have committed a transgression toward another person, we should reconcile our relationship with God first. When we approach God, we should leave nothing out. We are to take all of the sins we are responsible for in the break-down of a relationship with someone to Him and admit our sin. This chapter explains the confession process toward God as outlined in Scripture. When this properly occurs we will experience His full forgiveness and be ready to approach the other person we have transgressed.

A Typical Scenario

Have you ever been angry or upset because you received a traffic ticket that you perceived was unfair? Perhaps you described it to someone like this, "I am so angry and upset. The officer said I was reckless driving and gave me a ticket. Can you believe He said that I was eating a cheeseburger while I was driving? Well, you know what? I was. What's wrong that? A lot of people eat cheeseburgers while they're driving. Then, he said that I was texting, while I was eating the cheeseburger. Yeah, so what? I was texting, but I can still drive. You see, I can put my knees up on the wheel and drive that way. Oh, yes, he also wrote on the ticket that I had my dog on my lap which was distracting me. After I stopped texting, I used my electric shaver on my face. He must have been following me for a long time. How dare he give me a ticket? Doesn't he have anyone else to follow? There are a lot worse drivers out there than me. I certainly let that officer know how I felt about this ticket!"

Though the above is rather tongue-in-cheek rendering of a traffic ticket incident, it is meant to demonstrate how we often rationalize our mistakes, rather than admit them. We often try to figure out a way to get out of what we did that was wrong, instead of owning up to it and admitting that we had erred. This we must do!

A Scriptural Principle

The third principle in the reconciliation process is "we must fully repent of our sins and confess them before God." Often times, when we think of repentance, we may assume it simply means to be sorry for our sins. It actually has a fuller and broader meaning which encompasses three different aspects. True biblical repentance involves the admission of our sins, the sorrowing over those same transgressions, and the turning from those iniquities in a direction that is more righteous.

A Biblical Explanation

As God called us into His eternal kingdom, He first made us cognizant of our wretchedness and our sinfulness before Him. To become Christians, people had to proclaim sin and judgment to us, and we responded with repentance for that sin. This resulted from a real understanding of the absolute holiness of the Father, His Son, and the Spirit. As unsaved people, once we realized who Christ was, we came to fully understand just how unworthy and sinful we were before Him.

It is important to note that repentance does not end at the moment of salvation. True believers in Christ will constantly be recognizing the sins that they are committing and asking

God for forgiveness. This is not just an eternal issue but a relational one. When we received Christ as Savior and Lord, all of our sins were forgiven from the past, present, and future (Colossians 2:13-14; Romans 8:1). In our relationship with the Lord upon this earth in the flesh, we still confess our transgression. This restores our relationship with God in a relational sense and barriers are eliminated.

John speaks to this in his first letter. Some were saying in the church that they had matured to such a level that they no longer sinned in any way. John, the apostle, counters with a scathing response. In 1 John 1:8, the apostle emphatically states, "If we say that we have no sin, we deceive ourselves, and the truth is not in us." Then in verse 10, he declares, "If we say that we haven't sinned, we make him a liar, and his word is not in us." Those who claimed that they had never sinned or no longer sinned were simply lying to themselves, others, and God. The truth of His Word was not in them because this truth convicts us of sin.

Then sandwiched between these two convicting passages is what believers do when they realize they have sinned. In verse 9, he proclaims, "If we confess our sins, He is faithful and righteous to forgive us the sins, and to cleanse us from all unrighteousness." The verbs "confess" and "forgive" are in the present tense which indicates continual action in present time. Believers are continually confessing their sins, and God is continually forgiving them. Repentance and asking God to forgive us is a lifelong practice.

As we repent of our sins and experience God's constant forgiveness, then it becomes easier and easier to ask for the forgiveness of others we have transgressed. Also, it makes it much less difficult to accept the repentance of others as they transgress us. As saints, we must recognize our sinfulness or we might be destined to become angry, judgmental people.

This is exactly the point the Lord made in Matthew 7:1-5. Here Jesus spoke against the self-righteous attitudes of the Pharisees. They thought they were keeping the law perfectly and became bitter, angry, and judgmental critics of people. Jesus makes this pronouncement in verses 1-2, "Don't judge, so that you won't be judged. For with whatever judgment you judge, you will be judged; and with whatever measure you measure, it will be measured to you." Then in verses 3-4, The Lord inquires, "Why do you see the speck that is in your brother's eye, but don't consider the beam that is in your own eye? Or how will you tell your brother, 'Let me remove the speck from your eye;' and behold, the beam is in your own eye." Then in verse 5, Jesus chastises all of them saying, "You hypocrite! First remove the beam out of your own eye, and then you can see clearly to remove the speck out of your brother's eye." The beam is their rejection of Christ.

The Lord is explaining to them that they need to be taking care of their own sins first before they begin looking at the sins of another. The implication for us is astounding. As we constantly come in repentance before God and continually experience His grace, mercy, and love in forgiveness, it will create hearts in us that do the same for others. It will become easier for us to graciously and lovingly ask for forgiveness and mercifully and lovingly grant forgiveness to others. This in turn will make us people who are not so quick to judge the actions of others and condemn them. This passage is not banning judgment of any kind toward others; instead, it is requiring us to judge our own thoughts, words, actions, and attitudes first. This brings constant repentance.

As mentioned earlier, there are actually three aspects to the full concept of "repentance" in the Scripture. These are presented in various places by different writers in the New Testament. Repentance involves admitting the sins we have committed, sorrowing and mourning over their wickedness, and turning away from them toward righteousness. All of these are crucial elements in the repentance process and are expected and anticipated as the Spirit convicts us of our sin.

The first is the admission of sin. To fully repent, we must admit that we have sinned. This means that Christians are to acknowledge that the thoughts, words, and actions that they had taken were indeed sins. Notice 1 John 1:9 again, "If we confess our sins, He is faithful and righteous to forgive us the sins, and to cleanse us from all unrighteousness." John, the apostle, uses a critical word to explain his meaning. The Greek word translated "confess" literally means "to say the same thing." Our confession is to say the same thing about a thought, word, or action that God says about them. They are sinful. They are against God's law.

When Jesus encountered a rich young ruler, he claimed to have kept the whole law from his youth up (Mark 10:17-31; Matthew 19:16-30; Luke 18:18-30). Could that be true? No, the rich young ruler simply refused to admit his sin. To him every single thought, word, and action from his youth up was righteous. So Jesus told him to sell all he had which he refused to do. This manifested the real sin in his heart which was not displayed outwardly - greed. The Lord immediately exposed the iniquity which was deep within his heart and he would not admit this was sinful.

Instead, this wealthy young ruler left Jesus with his self-righteousness and wealth intact but not saved. Kingdom people always admit their sin and ask for forgiveness on a regular basis. We must stand before the Lord God and tell him the thoughts, words, and actions we have committed and agree with Him that they were sinful and violated His law. As we do this, we are to hold nothing back that the Lord brings to our minds. Of course, He does not expect us to remember or even know all that we may have done.

The second aspect of repentance is to mourn over those sins. In the Beatitudes, the Lord Jesus speaks of the spiritual characteristics of His children. Though these qualities appear physical, they really refer to spiritual aspects of his kingdom people. In Matthew 5:3, Jesus declares, "Blessed are the poor in spirit, for theirs is the kingdom of God." There is no virtue in being poor. He was speaking of those poor in their spirit. The Greek word translated "poor" means "bankrupt" and refers to the acknowledgement that His people know they are spiritually bankrupt in sin. This is the first aspect, we just discussed.

The Lord continues in verse 4, "Blessed are those who mourn, for they shall be comforted." This remark speaks of mourning over our bankrupt condition before God as one mourns over the dead. It refers to a deep sorrow over our sin and wickedness which is the second aspect. When someone receives the Lord, they admit their sin and mourn, grieve, and sorrow over it. As we live our Christians lives, we will be constantly convicted of our sins and are to admit them to the Lord. Then we will experience a grieving process when we fully face what we did. There is sorrow and mourning over it.

In 1 Corinthians, Paul describes the sins and difficulties this church encountered because they had been prideful and rebellious. The apostle Paul was so deeply hurt because the church had taken a stand against him. False prophets had risen up and found a leader in the church. This sinful leader with most of the church stood against Paul, the apostle, and his ministry.

As a result, the apostle was forced to send a difficult and confrontational letter which is referred to in 2 Corinthians 2:3-4. When he finally visited, they did not respond well. So, he shortened his visit and departed. Later, Paul sent Titus to discover their final response to his letter of rebuke. When Titus returned, he brought wonderful news of the church's repentance for their evil stand (2 Corinthians).

In 2 Corinthians 7:9, Paul vividly described the extent of their sorrow, grief, and mourning over their sin. He wrote, "I now rejoice, not that you were made sorry, but that you were made sorry to repentance. For you were made sorry in a godly way, that you might suffer loss by us in nothing." He spoke of their godly sorrow which produces the repentance leading to salvation. This is the sorrow Christians have when they come to Christ and every day of their lives thereafter. He contrasts this with another in verse 10, "For godly sorrow works repentance to salvation, which brings no regret. But the sorrow of the world works death." The first sorrow leads to initial salvation and the other to final eternal damnation. The other is a sorrow but not a godly one. It leads to despair and guilt-ridden anguish.

The first is the sorrow expressed by the woman who came to Jesus in Luke 7:37-39. This grieving woman washed His feet with her many tears and wiped them with her hair in sorrow over her sin! Then, she kissed His feet and anointed them with expensive perfume. What humility and mourning over wrongdoing! The second sorrow produces bitterness, despair, anger, and pride. It desires to lash out at others for hurting them, rebuking them, or interrupting their sin. This emotion vents at oneself in punishment and self-hatred. It will not admit sin and plead for forgiveness.

The third aspect in repentance is the repentance of sins. Though this word is used with a fuller meaning in defining the entire concept, it also has a unique meaning of its own. The Greek word translated "repent" means "to turn around in the opposite direction or change one's mind or behavior." We must turn around from our confessed sins and move in the opposite direction. We must commit ourselves to living differently. Luke records Peter's denial of even knowing the Lord in Luke 22:62 and how the apostle wept in sorrow and remorse afterward. Later, Luke records in Acts numerous sermons that Peter preached in great boldness for Christ. Peter clearly demonstrated that he had fully turned in the opposite direction from that sin. Of course, the Holy Spirit will provide the strength needed in order to accomplish this supernatural feat (Acts 2:4; Romans 8:13). Now, consider the response of Judas. In Matthew 27:3-9, he would not repent nor humble himself before the Lord Jesus and remove the guilt and sorrow through salvation. Instead, he simply killed himself to alleviate them from his life. This is the sorrow unto death.

As we interlace the three principles we have studied in these initial chapters, we clearly see how we are to reconcile our relationship with the Lord, before we can reconcile with others. The response of all believers when they have sinned against another will be to turn toward God first and ask Him for forgiveness. This is accomplished through the admission of their wrongs, sorrow over their sin, and a turning toward righteousness while leaving no sin in the transgression out. This is how we are to reconcile with God, our Father.

An Ancient Portrait

This repentance process is distinctly seen in the story of Achan's sin in the book of Joshua, chapters 6-8. Joshua was the commander of the nation of Israel after Moses died. He brought God's people to the land of Canaan. He was told by God to wipe out the people in this wicked land. This was due to the horrible atrocities of the Canaanites. These people were so extremely wicked that even their possessions were unclean. No one was to take any plunder in the battles. Only gold and silver and a few other items were to be collected for the Lord's house. God was very serious about protecting the purity of His people and standing against their evil.

The first city to be defeated in their quest was Jericho. As most know, the walls came down through a miraculous feat of the Lord, and the city was taken. Now it was time to move on to a place called Ai. Having sent out spies, they realized this would require a small army to conquer them. So their leader Joshua would only need 3000 men, not the normal 30,000. The army closed in on Ai with great expectations of a mighty victory.

Instead, the people of Ai ran them off killing 36 men and causing Israel to retreat in humiliating terror. Where was the power of the Lord God? What had happened? Something had gone terribly wrong. Joshua threw himself before the ark and begged the Lord to tell him what had happened. He was fearful that once the Canaanites heard of their miserable defeat, they would be run out of the country. The Lord told Joshua that one of his people had taken items from the city that was to be devoted solely to the Lord. The commander would have to find the violator and cleanse the nation from this atrocity. The Lord Himself would point him out, so all would know the seriousness of obeying the commandments of God Almighty, the God of Israel.

God told Joshua to bring the people before the Lord the next morning, and He would identify the transgressor. First, each tribe of the nation was brought before the Lord, and the Lord God singled out the tribe. Then He divided the tribe into smaller and smaller groups until He arrived at Achan and his family. So this man Achan was required by Joshua to stand before God Almighty and give Him glory and honor by admitting the sinful action he had taken. This is so crucial to our understanding of how to reconcile with God.

The admission of our wrongdoing glorifies the Lord God by recognizing His sovereignty and power over all people. Then Achan admitted his transgression in detail. In Joshua 7:20, the author recorded, "Achan answered Joshua, and said, 'I have truly sinned against Yahweh, the God of Israel, and this is what I have done.'" Notice, Achan admits he has broken God's law and sinned against God first. Then Achan describes exactly how he had sinned in verse 21. He explains this, "When I saw among the plunder a beautiful Babylonian robe, two hundred shekels of silver, and a wedge of gold weighing fifty shekels, then I coveted them and took them. Behold, they are hidden in the ground in the middle of my tent, with the silver under it."

Notice what the man did not do. He did not demonstrate any mourning over what he had done or committed himself and his family to living righteously from then on. He did not fully reconcile with God. Also, he did not reconcile with the people of Israel or Joshua. They had lost thirty-six lives and experienced a major defeat. Instead, he admits what he did, shows them where the possessions are hidden, and accepts the punishment. It appears that there was no repentance, mourning, and turning toward righteousness.

All of us deserve physical death the very first time we sin and every time after that (Romans 3:26). Yet, God displays tremendous mercy on us all. At other times, the Lord God determines that He will not show His mercy and grace in withholding physical death to teach His people an important lesson. This was one of those times. The perpetrators of this atrocity against God's holiness were taken out and stoned to death. All their possessions, including the possessions they had taken, were burned with their bodies. Then a heap of rocks were put over it as a memorial in order to teach future generations the utter seriousness of obeying the Lord God and honoring His holiness.

When we sin against others, sometimes we rationalize our actions and will not admit what we did, mourn over it, and turn the other way. This is not how God deals with us. We must stop the rationalization, and make things right with the Lord which honors and glorifies Him. Once our relationship with Him is fully reconciled, we will be ready to reconcile with those we have wronged. These steps are critical in the forgiveness process.

A Modern Anecdote

Sometime ago, a young man entered my counseling office with his parents because they thought he seemed depressed and sad. Since he was twenty-three (an adult), I had to bid the parents goodbye. This young man had been through a difficult time growing up after his parents divorced. He had to live rotating weeks with each parent which made him miserable. The mother periodically dated a series of men he did not like and the father married what he characterized as a cold and harsh woman.

Needless to say, the young man was not happy in either of these places. Whenever he spent time with his family, he was depressed and sad. Whenever he spent time with his friends he was happy and funny. This was an important bit of information worth noting. After some sessions, it became obvious that he had failed to launch. The mother was strong and demanding and the father had barely noticed him. His opinion about issues that affected him did not matter to either parent. So he developed the attitude that he would just "go with the flow."

Rather than asserting himself, he merely complied. This gave him a sense of imprisonment and a lack of control over anything. As a result, he became extremely dependent upon both his parents. As he continually acquiesced, the young man was unable to develop a real concept of himself and a hope for the future. He blamed his failure to launch on the fact that his mother needed him. How did he come up with this idea? As the men flowed in and out, the son basically fulfilled the role of her husband (not sexually, of course, but emotionally).

She took him places and did things only adults would do. Though he did not desire to go to coffee after a movie and talk about it, he did love feeling and acting like an adult. Yet, when decisions had to be made concerning buying clothes, or music, his school and social life, she made them. He was acting like her mother's husband in some areas and like a younger child in other areas. The two eventually developed an unnatural dependence on each other.

First, the mother had lost her husband and replaced him with her son. This is fairly common, and usually the parent is not even cognizant of the issue. God's blueprint embedded within a person is for he or she to be married (Genesis 2:18) with the exception of being singularly devoted to the Lord which Paul calls a "gift" (1 Corinthians 7:7, 32-34). When a spouse leaves, the blueprint does not automatically shut off.

Instead, one must replace the spouse with the Lord, not a child or a "live-in" partner (Psalm 68:4-6). Second, the young man should follow the Lord's blueprint "to leave and cleave" (Genesis 2:24) or be single and live a life devoted to Christ. The Lord never intended for children to be living with their parents beyond the childhood years of life (Proverbs 22:6; Ephesians 6:4). Third, the father was distant and unwilling to raise his son in the many things of the Lord and prepare him for manhood. On the other hand, his wife was inciting and exasperating his son until he would finally give into whatever she wanted (Ephesians 6:4).

Once this was discovered, it became time to reconcile the relationships and launch this young man into adulthood. This begins with repentance before the Lord. His mother had to be gently confronted for her mistakes. She had "to cut the umbilical cord" with her son both as her servant-child and as her surrogate husband. His father and step-mother had to be lovingly confronted for not taking the responsibility for teaching the son how to become a man and for exasperating him to the point of subservience to their every wish. Both mom and dad had to take responsibility for their divorce and his resultant predicament.

The son had to be confronted concerning his response to everything that had happened. The son had not assumed any adult responsibilities and launched himself from the nest. Instead, he had taken great advantage of the situation by relying upon the mother to meet the needs that a wife should have met or he should have taken care of himself as a single man (e.g. preparing food, laundry, earning a living, cleaning up after himself). All responded according to their own unique timeline (not all respond immediately).

All of them mourned over their transgressions and turned from them. Then, they committed themselves to moving in a more righteous direction. So, they began the critical process of restoration with each other. Sometimes, this takes a long time and at other times a short amount of time. It depends largely on the hard work and open hearts of all involved as the Holy Spirit works. Eventually, the young man's sadness and depression began to depart and were replaced with a new enthusiasm for his future. Finally, the son was able to launch into adulthood as a single man by finding a place to live. The launching of the young man's new adult life began with the entire family taking responsibility for their actions and admitting to the mistakes and sins each had done to the other members in the family.

A Personal Response

Dear Heavenly Father,

Though I have admitted my transgressions against You and (add name), I realize I have not taken them seriously. Help me to truly mourn over what I have done. Then, give me the desire to make a real commitment to the right kinds of actions. I want to be holy like You. I am sorry for breaking Your law. May I honor and glorify You in my relationship with (add name). I pray this in the name of Jesus. Amen.

Chapter 4

Accept God's Forgiveness

When we have sinned against another, we should begin the reconciliation process by approaching God. A Christian's relationship with Him has been damaged, and God must be dealt with first. To restore the relationship with Him, we are to spread out our transgressions before Him and take full responsibility for them. We are to admit that they are wrong and ask Him for forgiveness. The next step is to accept God's forgiveness with a sense of blessing and gratefulness.

A Typical Scenario

Suppose you suddenly awoke in the middle of the night and felt the full weight and burden of all your transgressions against God. Every sin you had committed started parading through your mind, and you began to write them down. You were completely honest and left nothing out. Wouldn't you write and write and write and write until your hand was so sore you could no longer hold the pen? Of course, I would too. Here is an important truth: since we are Christians, our long list of sins, transgressions, and iniquities from small to great have been forgiven! All of them are completely gone. It is important that we accept this by faith.

A Scriptural Principle

The fourth principle is "we must believe by faith that all our sins are forgiven in Jesus Christ with a sense of blessing and thankfulness." The moment we repented and received

Jesus Christ, all our past, present, and future sins and the punishment involved were washed away. What do I mean by this? At the very moment that we placed our faith in Jesus Christ, the penalty for all our sins paid at the cross was appropriated to us directly. Eternal life became ours with full, complete, and total forgiveness. Since this is a spiritual process, there may not have been a great feeling of relief or a tremendous sense of forgiveness at this defining moment in our lives. Instead, we should claim this forgiveness by faith.

A Biblical Explanation

To fully accept this forgiveness in our lives graciously and thankfully, we should understand exactly what happened at the cross. When we speak of forgiveness, we are speaking of two kinds of forgiveness. One concerns what occurred when we received Christ as Savior and Lord. Here the penalty that was paid was appropriated to us, our sins were forgiven, and we were declared righteous before God (Romans 8:1). The second occurs in our earthly relationship and fellowship with God and occurs as we confess our sins and ask Him for forgiveness (1 John 1:9). When I sin against my wife with an unkind word or action, she often forgives me even as I am sinning. Then, when I do go to her and ask for forgiveness and she grants it again (in a sense), all the barriers between us are removed. The relationship is fully restored because we each did our part and took our responsibility. Then I feel a great sense of blessing and gratefulness for her continual love, mercy, and grace. When the reverse happens she feels the same.

After David had sinned against God by taking Bathsheba and murdering her husband, the king wrote psalms 32 and 51. In these two psalms he has this relational forgiveness in mind. In Psalm 32:1-2, he rejoiced, "Blessed is he whose disobedience is forgiven, whose sin is covered. Blessed is the man to whom Yahweh doesn't impute iniquity, in whose spirit there is no deceit." He was overjoyed with a sense of blessing for God's forgiveness of Him. This blessing was accompanied by a sense of gratefulness. In Psalm 51:8, He alludes to this when he cries, "Let me hear joy and gladness, that the bones which you have broken may rejoice." Then in verse 10, he continues, "Create in me a clean heart, O God. Renew a right spirit within me." In verse 12, he entreats, "Restore to me the joy of your salvation. Uphold me with a willing spirit." Then in verse 14-15, he says, "Deliver me from the guilt of bloodshed, O God, the God of my salvation. My tongue shall sing aloud of your righteousness." He adds, "Lord, open my lips. My mouth shall declare your praise." How can one not feel the sense of blessing and gratefulness he experiences as he confesses his sins to the Lord?

Did David know God had already forgiven Him for all His sins? Of course he did. In fact, the prophet Nathan had confirmed this very fact when he was confronted by him. In 2 Samuel 12:13, when David declared that he had sinned, Nathan responded, "Yahweh also has put away your sin." Though David knew he was forgiven from a salvation point of view, he needed his relationship with God fully restored and deeply desired the sense of blessing and thankfulness that pours out of a true confession. We all know the sense of relief and joy that comes when we have fully admitted our sin, mourned over it, and turned from it. This is important because from this sense of blessing and thankfulness comes the willingness on our part to forgive ourselves, others, and, if necessary, to be humble enough to ask for forgiveness.

To fully comprehend this forgiveness leading us to accept it, producing blessing and thanksgiving, and stimulating us to forgive ourselves and others, we must understand the full extent of what Christ actually did. The second person of the

Trinity entered humanity for the purpose of dying for man's sins. The Father punished Jesus, the God-Man, instead of us to satisfy His just and holy wrath. God has no wrath toward us for the sins we now commit toward Him or others. God will still discipline us in His deep love as a Father (Hebrews 12:7), but He will no longer punish us in His holy wrath as a Judge (Romans 8:1).

Paul deepens our concept of what happened on the cross in Colossians 2. In verses 13-14, Paul explained, "You were dead in your trespasses and the uncircumcision of your flesh. He made you alive together with him, having forgiven us all our trespasses, wiping out the certificate of debt which was decrees against us; and he has taken it out of the way, nailing it to the cross" (DEJ). Christ has taken the certificate of debt consisting of decrees against us, and has nailed them to the cross. What are these "decrees?" The decrees are the many judgments against us for every transgression we ever committed, are committing, or will ever commit.

Standing before a righteous and wrathful God, we would have been judged and punished for all eternity. How many decrees against us would we have with a lifetime of sinning? More than we could possibly count! Our iniquities were paid for by our Lord Jesus Christ in his death and nailed to His cross. In Hebrews 9:22, the author of Hebrews declares in the final part of the verse, "Apart from shedding of blood there is no remission." Through the shed blood of the Lord, these sins and decrees were nailed to the cross and wiped away.

After our confession, we claim this great truth by faith and accept His forgiveness. In Romans 4:8, Paul explains our blessed state when he testifies, "Blessed is the man whom the Lord will by no means charge with sin." There is the sense of blessing and gratefulness. God, our Father, will not charge us with our sin. We merely accept this. In Hebrews 8:12, the author says, "For I will be merciful to their unrighteousness. I will remember their sins and lawless deeds no more." Here he quotes Jeremiah 31:34, where God is directly speaking. Then in Hebrews 10:17, the author repeats, "I will remember their sins and their iniquities no more." In verse 22, the holy writer compares our full forgiveness to washing with pure water, "Let's draw near with a true heart in fullness of faith, having our hearts sprinkled from an evil conscience, and having our body washed with pure water." As saints confess their sins, they can imagine pure water flowing over them washing their sins away. If this truth does not bring a sense of blessing and thankfulness, what will?

The same concept can be seen in the Old Testament when the prophets speak of God washing away or removing the sins of His people Israel after they had confessed, mourned, and turned from their sin. In Isaiah 38:17, Hezekiah says, "Behold, for peace I had great anguish, but you have in love for my soul delivered it from the pit of corruption." Then, he adds, "For you have cast all my sins behind your back." As believers accept God's forgiveness, they will experience a blessing and gratefulness of God casting those sins behind His back. In Isaiah 43:25, God emphatically pronounces, "I, even I, am he who blots out your transgressions for my own sake; and I will not remember your sins." The Lord directly speaks about blotting out their sins and remembering them no more. In Isaiah 44:22, the Lord asserts, "I have blotted out like a dark cloud your transgressions, and like a thick mist your sins. Return to me, for I have redeemed you" (DEJ). In this passage, God explains His redemption of His people as having "blotted out" their sins.

In Psalm 85:2, the sons of Korah cry out with praise, "You have forgiven the iniquity of your people. You have covered all their sin." In Micah 7:19, the holy prophet describes what will happen to the sins of God's people when they turn back to Him, "He will again have compassion on us. He will tread our iniquities under foot; and you will cast all their sins into the depths of the sea." As you and I come before the throne of grace and repent of the sins we have committed in a relationship, we can know that God has covered over them, treaded their iniquities under His foot, and cast them into the depths of the sea. Will this not prepare us to accept the Lord's forgiveness, and then to forgive ourselves, others, or humbly ask for forgiveness?

Lastly, we must understand the abundant grace that was bestowed on us because the Lord will require us to bestow the same to ourselves and others. In Ephesians 1:7-8, Paul portrays what Jesus accomplished in these words, "In whom we have our redemption through his blood, the forgiveness of our trespasses, according to the riches of his grace, which he made to abound toward us in all wisdom and prudence." Notice what the apostle states concerning God's grace. The words "made to abound" is only one Greek word meaning "to exceed a fixed number of measure, to be over, abundant, excelling beyond." His grace overflowed exceedingly beyond anything that could be measured in order to forgive. Notice it is "according to the riches of His grace." Paul did not say "out of" but "according to" the riches of His grace. This grace is infinite having no bounds, and this makes His forgiveness infinite and without bounds. The word "riches" is a Greek word meaning "riches, wealth." According to the great and abundant wealth of His grace came forgiveness. It came when we received Christ. Moment by moment as we confess our sins, He forgives and forgives and forgives again and again until our very redemption.

We desperately need His "wealth of grace" because we not only sin repeatedly but commit some horribly grievous sins against God, ourselves, and others. Yet, God forgives all of them. There is not one sin that a believer can commit that was not dealt with on the cross of Christ. When we repent and accept this forgiveness, a tremendous sense of blessing and thankfulness pours forth from our lives. In Psalm 103:1-2, the psalmist testifies, "Bless the Lord, O my soul, And all that is within me, bless His holy name. Bless the Lord, O my soul, And forget none of His benefits." This sense of blessing results from all of the benefits that God bestows on us as His people. In the first part of verse 3, he mentions forgiveness, "Who pardons all your iniquities."

The psalms continue with this incredible theme. In Psalm 106:1, the writer articulates his sense, "Praise Yahweh! Give thanks to Yahweh, for he is good, for his loving kindness endures forever." What could be kinder than forgiveness? In verse 47, the writer communicates, "Save us, Yahweh, our God, gather us from among the nations, to give thanks to your holy name, to triumph in your praise!" Salvation for the nation was the forgiveness of their sins and the deliverance from captivity of their enemies on earth, our salvation is the forgiveness of our sins and the deliverance from hell for all eternity. Temporally, it is the deliverance from the weight and guilt of our sins and the restoration of our relationship with God.

In Psalm 28:7, David testifies of his thanksgiving, joy, and blessing, "Yahweh is my strength and my shield. My heart has trusted in him, and I am helped. Therefore my heart greatly rejoices. With my song I will thank him." In verse 8, he adds, "Yahweh is their strength. He is a stronghold of salvation to his anointed." What a sense of blessing and thanksgiving! Yet, the Lord God does not want His children to stop right there. He wants us to take our experience of blessing and to pour out forgiveness upon ourselves and others. Also, as our hearts are full of all His blessings, we must use it to motivate ourselves to humbly go before those we have transgressed and ask for forgiveness, if necessary.

An Ancient Portrait

A great example of this sense of blessing and gratefulness is seen in Luke chapter seven. When Jesus was in Galilee, the Lord was invited into the house of a Pharisee named Simon. At times, Pharisees would persuade the Lord to give a talk in their homes to various dignitaries. Sometimes, He was invited for the purpose of trapping Him in something He said. Other times, they were serious about His ministry and message and wanted to learn from Him. While Jesus was at Simon's table, a woman who had the reputation among the Jews of being a "sinner" (most likely a prostitute), entered the house with a jar of expensive oil. I am sure to everyone's amazement she began to wet the feet of the Lord with her tears and wipe them with her hair.

After this, she kissed Christ's feet and anointed Him with her oil. One would think that Simon and the others would be filled with empathy and compassion as they saw this poor woman kneeling before Christ. Instead, these religious men of Israel were stunned that Jesus even allowed such a sinner to touch Him. "Why did He have anything to do with her?" they must have thought. The scoffers viewed the entire scene with disgust. They reasoned that if this Jesus was truly the prophet He claimed to be, He would know how wretched that woman was.

They did not realize that she was in the middle of an act of deep repentance crying out for ultimate forgiveness. Her tears were her repentance, her anointing was her recognition of His Deity, and His acceptance was His forgiveness. As she experienced His forgiveness, her tears began to flow from her sense of acceptance, blessing, and thankfulness. To open up Simon and the others' minds to the significance of the moment, Jesus told him the story of a lender who had two people who owed him money. One of the two owed him five hundred denarii (500 day's wages) and the other five denarii (5 day's wages). The lender then forgave them both. One was forgiven a large amount and the other a smaller amount. Then Jesus asked Simon to pick the person who would love this lender more. Simon responded that it would be the one with the larger amount.

The implication was obvious. This woman, who was such a sinner, was showing a greater love for Jesus because Jesus had forgiven a greater amount of her sins than others. What a testimony of His forgiveness and her love demonstrated through repentance, acceptance, and gratefulness! Then the Lord Jesus turned the tables on Simon and compared his treatment of the Lord with her conduct toward Him. He was a self-proclaimed righteous man, and she was a proclaimed sinner. Christ told Simon that he did not wash the Lord's feet when He entered his home (a custom due to the wearing of sandals), but this woman washed them with her tears and wiped them dry with her hair. Simon did not kiss the Lord when He arrived (a common greeting at that time), but the woman continually kissed His feet. Simon did not anoint the head of the Lord with oil (a common custom to remove the smell of travel, like perfume), but she anointed His feet. The implication was clear. Here is a simple contrast between her humility and care for Christ and Simon's distaste of Jesus.

Then the Lord pronounced His forgiveness of the many sins of the woman. He acknowledged her great love for Him as Savior and Lord. Then Jesus declared exactly what had happened. He had given her the very gift she had desired all along which was forgiveness. Now Simon and his guests would clearly understand what they were viewing. Christ demonstrated through this story the love and forgiveness He has for us, and the sense of blessing and thankfulness we are to have for Him. She was welcomed, and we are welcomed. She repented and found forgiveness, and we repent and find the same forgiveness. She greatly sinned and found pardon, and we greatly sin and find the same pardon.

When we come before our Lord and Savior in repentance, sorrow, and confession, we will receive complete and total forgiveness every single time. We received it all on the cross eternally, now we receive it all relationally. We merely have to accept it all with blessing and thankfulness. Then out of that experience of full forgiveness, we must go to those who have transgressed us and demonstrate that same forgiveness toward them. To those we have transgressed, we must show the same repentance. We must display that same forgiveness toward ourselves. What a God of forgiveness we have! Now we must show it through our own forgiveness of others.

A Modern Anecdote

A young lady came into my office one day after spending weeks in rehab for a drug addiction. She told me that though she had learned some good things at the center, it had still left her empty inside. She was clean but empty. She told me that she did not know where to go from this point. The young woman went to her pastor who often refers clients to me, and she was referred. She told me that she needed God and had heard that I could help her find Him. Her story was a tragic one. She described herself, her mom, and her dad as the perfect little family living in a huge country home in the Midwest.

While her mom stayed home and took care of the house, her father was one of the managers of an equipment rental company. As a girl, she was good in school and won many achievement awards. She could not remember one time that her parents had argued or exchanged unkind words. From her perspective all was well and comfortable in her world.

Then one day when she was about eleven, her dad came home and said he had lost his job. Her mom and dad went into their room and had a terrible argument which she had never seen before. She was petrified. The police came later that night and hand-cuffed her dad and took him away. When she asked mom what had happened, she explained that her father had stolen a huge amount of money from the company to pay back gambling debts. Her mom had never worked a day in her life and did not know what to do. After a year, her parents divorced, and her life felt like it was over. Since her father had mortgaged the house to pay attorney's fees, there was no equity left. As a result, they sold the house for a loss and had nothing left. They were going to have to live with her grandparents in a big city. She told me she felt like she was living in a bad movie.

At twelve, her world shattered. She felt as if it had gone from a picture perfect home to a dirty little house in a dirty suburb where the lawns were brown and the people were tough. The school was old and loud, and no one would talk to her. Then one day a druggy-type girl befriended her. This girl taught her how to fit in. She took her shopping for cooler clothes, showed her how to do her hair and make-up, and introduced her to drugs and older more mature boys. From that day forward, it was one party after another, while her mother worked long hours. In high school, she was almost always high on drugs. Her relationship with her mother deteriorated until one night she just stormed off and never returned. After two husbands divorced her and three of her children were removed by social services, she decided it was time to get cleaned up.

The woman was twenty-nine and empty. Now, she was sitting in my office asking for help. So, I shared the good news of Jesus Christ with her. Our Lord God was willing to accept her with open arms in spite of what she had done. He was willing to forgive all her sins and rebuild her life into the beautiful image of His Son. The Lord would give her a new identity, a new family of God, and help her go back and reconcile with all of those she had hurt and had hurt her. When she came for the next session, she explained that she could not believe that God would forgive her. She felt she was a total "screw-up" as she called it. I told her, "When you repent and receive Jesus Christ, you have to believe that God has forgiven you by faith with blessing and gratitude. You will make other mistakes as a Christian and will again have to accept this forgiveness by faith." We prayed and she received Jesus Christ as Savior and Lord. Then we began the process of rebuilding her life now in Jesus Christ.

A Personal Response

Dear Heavenly Father,

While I was reading this chapter, I suddenly realized that I have not fully accepted your forgiveness with a sense of blessing and thankfulness for the sins I have committed in my relationship with (add name). I am truly sorry. Father, please help me to claim your full forgiveness by faith. I struggle with this and want desperately to overcome it in Your power. May I honor and glorify You in my relationship with (add name). I do pray all of this in the name of Jesus. Amen.

Chapter 5

Forgive Yourself All

When we sin against another, before we go to them to ask for forgiveness, we must first approach God. We admit our sins and leave nothing out. We mourn over them and make a commitment to act in a more righteous way. With a sense of blessing and gratefulness, we accept God's forgiveness. After this, we must fully forgive ourselves. The Lord God may forgive us, but we do not always forgive ourselves. At times, when the memory of a sin rears its ugly head, we may experience all of the regret, shame, and humiliation again. Then we may beat ourselves up over and over again. This does not have to happen; we can overcome this in Christ. This is why He came to free us from sin's grip.

A Typical Scenario

Perhaps, you have had or even heard a conversation with a friend, parent, sibling, child, acquaintance, co-worker, or fellow student which went something like this, when they asked you how you were doing? You say or hear, "I am fine. I am just fine. Everything is going great. (Pause.) No, really, I am doing great. Yes, that was a big mistake, humiliating and embarrassing, but I am okay with it. (A moment of silence occurs). No, what am I saying, everything is not fine. I am miserable and depressed. I will never get over what I did. I hate myself. The embarrassment was horrible. I cannot bear it! Whatever I do reminds me of how rotten I am!

A conversation like this describes how we may feel when we commit a terrible sin against someone. There lies a heavy weight of humiliation and shame upon us. Even after the sin has been confessed, the memory keeps returning whenever we see or hear something similar, in a book, movie, song, or experience we have. This may go on for days, weeks, or even years. Christians do not have to live with this weary load and strain. God desires for us to experience full forgiveness which includes the full forgiving of ourselves for the sin.

A Scriptural Principle

The fifth critical principle in healing relationships is "we must forgive ourselves for our sin as God has forgiven us." Once we have accepted God's forgiveness, we must turn our attention toward ourselves, before we turn it toward others. It is very difficult to restore a relationship with someone else, when we are still dealing with the sin within ourselves. This will make us feel defeated, broken, and unable to build the relationship anew. We do not have to carry this burden; instead, we can be free of it once and for all. We can be fully released from these self-imposed chains. Notice, I said, "self-imposed!" This kind of bondage comes from within. It needs to be identified and then dealt with.

A Biblical Explanation

To unchain ourselves from the bonds of our own lack of forgiveness, we must understand the source of the shame, guilt, and humiliation we feel. This does not originate from the Lord Jesus Christ. Once we confess the sins and accept our forgiveness by faith, it should all flow away. If it does not, then the flesh is the culprit. In Romans 7:20, Paul calls our sinful flesh the "sin which dwells in me." The sin principle resides in our physical bodies. The flesh (common word for this principle) desires to wallow in its own sin. It can be prideful, arrogant, and boastful, but it can also be insecure, worried, and unable to trust God. In our case, it is the voice inside us that says, "You are no good, pathetic, and just plain stupid! You will never overcome this moronic act. You fool! You idiot!" It chastises us like a vicious parent. It whips saints with the memories of their own mistakes over and over again.

In 1 Corinthians 9, he uses a powerful boxing analogy to explain how he handled this ugly sin principle inside him. In verse 27, he describes it in these words, "But I beat my body and bring it into submission, lest by any means, after I have preached to others, I myself should be rejected." The word "beat" in the Greek means "to beat black and blue." In our case, it would refer to hard effort to fight back against the flesh's lies. When we begin to feel angry or pity toward ourselves for some past sins, we must realize this is not the "new us" but the "old us."

The flesh has two powerful accomplices in its endeavor to lie to us: the world (1 John 2:15) and the Devil (John 8:44). The world or society of unbelievers enjoys watching God's people fall from grace and then scoffing at them (Psalm 1:1). The Devil loves to find God's righteous people and then test their loyalty (Job 1:11), tempt them to sin (Luke 22:31), or else accuse them of evil day and night before the Lord God (Revelation 12:10). So believers must be aware of these two enemies coercing the flesh to lie and influencing Christians to become depressed, defeated, grief-stricken, angry, bitter, or immobilized about a transgression they have committed against other saints or even unbelievers. They do not regard reconciliation between people as a virtue.

This battle to overcome the guilt, shame, and humiliation of past actions pouring forth into full self-forgiveness can be fought using several biblical strategies. The first involves our minds. In our minds, we must "take every thought captive to Christ." In 2 Corinthians, Paul, the apostle, discussed the many false beliefs the saints possessed about him and their faith. Then in chapter 10, verse 5, he described his ultimate objective in all of his preaching and letter writing. He was "throwing down imaginations and every high thing that is exalted against the knowledge of God, and bringing every thought into captivity to the obedience of Christ."

This is a simple concept when examined carefully. Every single idea or thought should be examined. Those thoughts that are contrary to the Scriptures should be discarded and those consistent should be embraced. In Romans 12, Paul explains how Christians can resist conforming themselves to the world, and it involves their minds. In verse 2, Paul states this, "Don't be conformed to this world, but be transformed by the renewing of your mind." Our mind is renewed in God's Word by discarding worldly thoughts and embracing God's thoughts. This then transforms us into His image. Christians forgive themselves and do not carry around guilt, shame, and humiliation. They continually discard thoughts that condemn and embrace thoughts that forgive.

How is this practiced in our lives? We speak to ourselves identifying where the negative thoughts are coming from and replace them with new ones. I will often say to myself, "I know these thoughts are from my flesh. God has forgiven me according to 1 John 1:9. I will not believe that God will hold this against me." This is essentially what Christ did with the Devil in His temptation in the wilderness. The Devil tempted Him, and Jesus quoted Scripture (Matthew 4:1-11). When we are tempted through our flesh by a memory or some thought of our sin, we must stand against it by saying, "This is not the real me nor is it the Holy Spirit, I have been forgiven, and I will let it go. Please God help me to let it go. I discard the negative and embrace the positive.

Second, we must become strong in our faith that the Lord has forgiven us. We know we have full forgiveness of our sins at the cross eternally and the full forgiveness of our sins at confession relationally, now we must believe this critical truth intellectually and emotionally. Abraham was given a promise by the Lord God that was too fantastic to believe. After Sarah was past child-bearing years and they both were old, He told them Sarah would conceive a son and Abraham would have a true heir. This was so unbelievable to the both of them that their response was exactly the same. They responded by laughter (Genesis 17:17-19; 18:12). It was not laughter of joy but the laughter of hearing something so outrageous that it could not possibly be true. God's promise was fulfilled, and Isaac was born.

When we read in the Scriptures that God forgives all our sins, it appears wonderful and easy to believe. When we do something really wicked, shameful, or humiliating, then His forgiveness can seem so outrageous that it could not be true. Deep down in the recesses of our souls, we refuse to believe it. This is the same feeling Abraham and Sarah had. How did Abraham overcome this? Paul articulated what happened in Romans 4:18-21. He wrote, "Besides hope, Abraham in hope believed, to the end that he might become a father of many nations, according to that which had been spoken, 'So will your offspring be.'" When the Lord originally told Abraham that he would have offspring, he believed God based on His Word.

In verse 19, Paul delineates what Abraham thought when he considered all of the physical evidence, "Without being weakened in faith, he didn't consider his own body, already having been worn out, (he being about a hundred years old), and the deadness of Sarah's womb." Abraham looked at the evidence of their old bodies and was not weakened in faith. He discarded all thoughts from his flesh mocking him and telling him it was impossible. Instead, he grew stronger in faith. In verse 20, the apostle asserted, "Yet, looking to the promise of God, he didn't waver through unbelief, but grew strong through faith." Then his mind embraced the thoughts which were consistent with God's Word, "Giving glory to God, and being fully assured that what he had promised, he was also able to perform." Over and over God performed the promises He made because He has the power to do it. This was being embraced in his mind, as the Spirit was assuring Him of this truth. Then he glorified God.

How does this passage apply to us in forgiveness? God promised that as we received Him, He forgave us on the cross eternally. When we confess our sins to Him now, He forgives us relationally. When we consider the humiliation, guilt, and shame of some sin we committed, we discard the thoughts that God will not forgive us this time. We embrace the truth that the Lord God said He would forgive us, and has the power to do it. Then the Holy Spirit will assure us, and we will grow strong in faith.

The third way to overcome our own lack of forgiveness is guard our hearts and minds in Christ Jesus. Paul exhorts the Christians in Philippians 4:6-7 to never be anxious about anything. Instead, we are to bring everything to our God in prayer with thanksgiving. That "everything" includes the sense of disappointment and guilt over a sin against a loved one. He then promises the peace of God which will guard our hearts and thoughts in Christ Jesus. The next two verses are often left out of a discussion concerning the removal of anxiety but are equally important. After we pray and turn these requests to God, we must think and act differently.

In Philippians 4:8, Paul adds, "Finally, brothers, whatever things are true, whatever things are honorable, whatever things are just, whatever things are pure, whatever things are lovely, whatever things are of good report; if there is any virtue, and if there is any praise, think about these things." Then in verse 9, he concludes with a general statement, "The things which you learned, received, heard, and saw in me: do these things, and the God of peace will be with you." Once we turn our requests over to God, we must change our thinking and doing. Our minds must dwell on honorable, just, pure, lovely, virtuous, reputable, praise-worthy things, while we behave in a way that is consistent with Paul and the apostles (righteous ways). The result will be peace in our hearts and souls. This is a godly peace which will surpass any comprehension.

The fourth way to unchain ourselves from the bonds of our own lack of forgiveness is to deal with the memories of our sin. The memory system that God has imbedded in us was to learn from our mistakes. We put our hand in a fire and get burned. Through that painful experience, we make a memory. Then, we learn never to do this again. When we see the fire again, our memory of being burned returns, and we are warned. This will work exactly the same way with our sins. When we sin, we receive the consequences of our sin which might include shame, guilt, anguish, and humiliation before repentance. When we travel through our lives, many different triggers bring up those painful memories.

We will need to rehearse what was learned and recommit to our new behavior. These are reminders to be careful. They do not have to debilitate us. They will bring up some of the feelings we experienced when the problem occurred. This is what memory is supposed to do, so we do not forget how "burned" we got. I usually say to myself, "I am glad I went through that experience. I will never do that again because the guilt, shame, and humiliation were so great." I will thank the Lord Jesus Christ for His forgiveness and rejoice in my relationship with Him always.

An Ancient Portrait

A great illustration of this supernatural ability to forgive oneself is Peter (Matthew 26; Mark 14; Luke 22; John 18). In the Garden of Gethsemane, Jesus told His disciples that He was about to be betrayed, and all of them would fall away. Peter declared that he would never fall away. Jesus looked at Peter and told him directly that this very night before the cock crowed, Peter would deny Him three times. The apostle declared that he would die before he ever denied the Lord. Aren't we the exactly same way? At first, we think that we could never do some of the sins that others have done. Later, we find we have done the very same or similar thing.

This chief of the apostles could not even conceive of the fact that he would ever deny the Lord. Then the mob came. The leaders of the Jews dragged Jesus away. Peter followed Him to the courtyard of Annas, the former high priest. After he entered, a slave girl walked up to him and asked if he were one of the disciples of Jesus. Without hesitation, he denied that he even knew Jesus. Then Peter walked over and began to warm his hands in front of the fire. He was joined by some of the servants and officials. Again, he was asked if he knew Jesus. Again, Peter denied knowing Him. Finally, a servant of one of the officials noticed his accent. The servant proclaimed that not only did Peter have a Galilean accent but he had actually seen him with Jesus. Peter responded by cursing, swearing, and proclaiming loudly that he did not know the man. Peter had the accent and was seen with Jesus by an eye-witness, but He still lied.

After this, Peter was so distraught that he went out and wept bitterly. He was genuinely repentant and sorrowful for this wicked deed. I am sure he confessed it to God. When he was restored by Jesus in John 21:15, it is never brought up again. It is never mentioned in his letters or in the book of

Acts. Peter was a joy-filled, peace-filled, and thankful saint. He had accepted by faith his forgiveness and did not beat himself up over and over, or churn it over and over in his mind. Peter had found joy after his confessions. We can find the same. This does not mean there were no consequences to Peter's denial. It is written in all four gospels as a testimony to what Peter did. The greater testimony was the courage and boldness Peter displayed after his fall. He went on to achieve great things for God.

Peter never dwelt on his colossal failure, nor did he forget it because he never denied the Lord again. In fact, on many occasions he stood boldly for the Lord Jesus. In his letters, he spoke of the courage of the other men of faith to encourage his brothers and sisters to remain strong. He also remained in truth and practiced righteousness himself while trusting God that he too was fully forgiven. Once we are able to fully forgive ourselves, we can forgive those who transgressed us or ask for forgiveness of those that we transgressed.

A Modern Anecdote

In the world today, adultery has become a fairly common occurrence. This is a difficult situation for all involved. Some Christians think that adultery should always lead to divorce, but this simply is not the case. I have seen the Holy Spirit rebuild many marriages in which adultery occurred. A while ago, a married couple entered my counseling office in the pit of this debilitating situation. The wife was weeping, and the husband was completely distraught. He had been involved in a six month long affair, yet they both wanted to save the relationship.

As I was speaking to the husband, he began to shed tears and muttered, "Dr. Jones, I became that guy!" I asked him to explain what he meant by that comment. He told me that he was now "the guy that everyone in his community, church, job, and neighborhood, will stare at, talk about, and avoid." Unfortunately, this situation could and does actually occur, but it is a sin and transgression that can be forgiven (1 John 1:7; Colossians 2:13).

The husband was a very high ranking city official. Often, his office would take in a group of interns and provide the experience they needed to complete their university training. He usually wasn't involved directly with the interns, but the one in charge was in the hospital preparing for surgery. One particular female intern did catch his eye, but he reminded himself how happy he was in his marriage. Also, he knew the Lord was watching. She traveled with him from time to time as he continued his work in the city. Every time she returned to his office, she was dressed more provocatively.

Feelings were beginning to develop on both sides, until finally she suggested they stay a little longer at his office to finish the city project that they were working on together. They suggested that could order in dinner. He knew that everyone had gone home for the evening but gave into the temptation. This "working dinner" turned into a powerful romantic encounter leading to a six month affair. He told me that all along he had mixed feelings about what he was doing but continued with the affair anyway. The woman was unsaved, unmarried, and was not at all bothered by it.

Finally, the wife found a receipt from a hotel in his wallet and confronted him. The husband confessed everything, and the wife demanded that he leave. He said good-bye to his four shocked children and went to stay with a friend. After some time, she realized how much she loved him and asked him to return home. He already had ended the relationship with the other woman. Over the weeks, many issues came to light from his childhood including how he was raised and the difficulties his father had with the same issue, his habits surrounding his purity, their lack of intimacy, and his lack of adequate safeguards. Many people think, "Oh, I can trust my husband or wife." The issue is not trust, it is a healthy fear of the flesh, the world (society and their values), and the Devil, and the devastation one can experience when these enemies of our righteousness are left unguarded and unchecked.

After dealing with each and every one of these factors, the process of forgiveness and reconciliation had to begin. The obstacle that caused the largest problem was not the wife and his children forgiving him, it was his unwillingness to forgive himself. He was filled with anxiety because he felt like he was wearing a large sign that read "Adulterer!" which everyone could see. He began to think every conversation was about him, and every look was a look of condemnation. Even this he could handle as part of the consequences of what he had done, but his inner voice kept condemning him.

The inner voice that haunted him was not his new man but his old man: the flesh. To relieve him of this constant condemnation, I shared with him key biblical concepts in this chapter. This provided for him the truth that the Spirit utilized to remove the mental sign and to allow him to fully forgive himself. The final and most critical step for their marriage involved the placing of various safeguards into his life which would rebuild the trust of his wife and children and prevent this sin from occurring again.

The setting up of various safeguards (Philippians 3:1) will preserve his purity and the sanctity of their marriage bed (Hebrews 13:4). This is crucial in rebuilding the relationship. This will also aid in the forgiveness process of his wife and his children as they literally watch him demonstrate over and over his commitment to his purity before God and them.

A Personal Response

Dear Heavenly Father,

I recognize you are my sovereign Lord. As I was reading this chapter, I realized that I have not completely forgiven myself for the sins I have committed toward you and (add name). I am so sorry. Please help me forgive myself as You have already fully forgiven me. Help me to constantly honor and glorify You in my relationship with (add name). Give to me Your wisdom as I set up safeguards to prevent me from falling into this sin again. I pray this in the name of Jesus. Amen.

Conclusion

As we conclude this book, I would like to leave us with some final thoughts about our God of forgiveness and what His Son did on the cross for us. First, if we understand the full extent of what was wrought for us on that cursed tree in order to forgive us, it will become so much easier to do the same thing for others. Second, if you read this entire book and realized that you do not understand salvation or have never received Christ as Lord and Savior, then I would like to provide that opportunity. Please do not skip this section; it may be the most important in your life.

From all outward appearances, humans seem "good" and attempt to live decent lives. This is man's concept of himself. This is not God's concept. The Almighty's view is that people all over the world and throughout the ages sin, sin, and sin again (Romans 3:23). This is a terrible and utterly destructive condition. Yet, they have ramifications that are far worse. These sins condemn us to everlasting divine retribution.

Though described briefly in the Old Testament, the Lord Jesus Christ clearly announced and proclaimed the future punishment to come. Contrary to popular belief, Jesus did not only speak of love, grace, and mercy, He also spoke of the coming judgment for sin. He declared that the judgment of sin would be everlasting punishment in a place He called "Hell." The Lord portrayed this place as an eternal inferno (Matthew 18:8) where there would be the weeping (from the sorrow) and gnashing of teeth (from the agony and anguish of suffering) continually into eternity (Matthew 8:12; 13:42, 50; 22:13; 24:51; 25:30; Luke 13:28).

Why must people face this horrific punishment? Though God is a God of love, grace, and mercy, He is also a God of great holiness, righteousness, and justice (Psalm 89:14,18). These attributes are just as much a part of His divine nature as His love, grace, and mercy. You have broken God's law as we all have and the penalty must be paid. This began with the first man Adam (Genesis 3:1-7). When this occurred, His love, grace, and mercy surfaced and a provision was made. Someone else would have to take man's place and pay the penalty. Someone who had never transgressed Him, who would never deserve punishment, and would fulfill all of God's Laws, would be substituted in man's place. This was the Son of God, Jesus Christ.

As the God-Man, He would pay the penalty for our sins in His death on the cross. Once done, the Lord God made only one provision for people to appropriate what His Son had done on the cross for them. This provision is receiving Jesus Christ as Savior and Lord. Though I cannot possibly share with you this good news in the confines of this book, I would love for you to consider purchasing my book entitled, *Finding The Light: The Kingdom of Heaven and How To Enter It*. It can be found for sale on Amazon.com. It is inexpensive and contains the full gospel message for your consideration. This message is so important and extensive that it cannot adequately be contained in a few pages at the end of a book.

If you are a believer, you must go out into the world and forgive as you are forgiven. These principles are to be lived and shared with others. You now have the tools to make your relationships last a lifetime. Go live them out and share them with others!

ABOUT THE AUTHOR

Dr. Donald Jones is currently a Christian Pastoral Counselor with thirty-eight years of experience in the fields of pastoral ministry, public education, and Christian counseling. He carries degrees and certificates from four major universities and from a variety of educational institutions. He has been a professor of Languages and Bible, a television commentator, and a featured speaker at a variety of events and seminars at churches, schools, and other organizations across the United States. He is a member in good standing of several secular and Christian professional organizations. Dr. Jones has been a published author since 1976. For further information view his website at www.donjonesphd.com.

www.ingramcontent.com/pod-product-compliance
Lightning Source LLC
Chambersburg PA
CBHW031525040426
42445CB00009B/407